This Candlewick book
belongs to:

_____

_____

_____

WRIGGLE AND BUZZ: MY FIRST BOOK OF

BUGS

SIMON MOLE

ILLUSTRATED BY ADAM MING

CANDLEWICK PRESS

CONTENTS

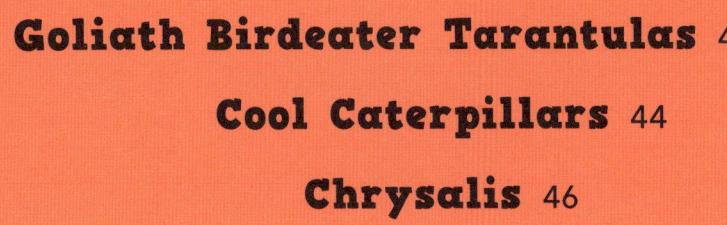

ABOUT THIS BOOK

The first animal to walk on land was a bug. The first animal to fly through the sky was also a bug. And today, for every human on Earth, there are over 1.4 billion bugs! Bugs have been around since before the time of the dinosaurs, and you can still find them now in every corner of the globe.

We definitely need insects and other tiny critters more than they need us. Without them, most flowers and plants would die out. This would mean that lots of bigger animals, including humans, wouldn't have as much food to eat. Also, there'd be steaming piles of poop everywhere! (More on that later.)

As well as playing an important part of life on Earth, bugs are also brilliantly beautiful, delightfully disgusting, and wonderfully weird. In these pages, you'll meet some of the coolest critters on the planet—from huge, bird-eating spiders that hunt alone in the rainforest to tiny termites that work together to build mud towers that stand taller than giraffes.

Take a look at the bugs on this page. Maybe you can spot some you already know. Are there any you'd like to know more about?

If so, you're in the right place!

MEET THE BUGS

MILLIPEDES

The first step (and the second and the third)

WAS US!

The first step (and the second and the third).

Who was the first animal to ever walk on land,

over four hundred million years ago?

The first to crawl out of the ocean and onto the sand?

It was us! The millipedes! Now you know!

The first step (and the second and the third)

WAS US!

The very first feet to walk on this Earth.

AFRICAN DRIVER ANTS

Keep in step and move along!
Twenty million move as one!

Keep in step, keep stepping hard!
Hungry hunters on the march.

If it moves, it won't survive—
we eat anything alive!

Wasps and beetles, slugs and worms,
rats and crabs, and snakes and birds.

Swarm and smother, rip and tear—
don't stop till there's nothing there.

Now you know our marching song,
keep in step and move along!

SPRINGTAILS

I am as small as this period.
But the spring in my tail
is so strong—
flicks so quick—
it catapults me up
away from danger.
Backflip after backflip,
spinning thirty times faster
than a helicopter blade at top speed!

WHEEEEEEE

EEEEEEEEEEEEEEEEEEEEE!

MONARCH BUTTERFLIES

We wake up for the first time
and already know how to get there,
like a magical map in our minds.
Nobody told us. We just know.

We just . . .

        We just . . .

                We just **go!**

Three thousand miles to the mountains of Mexico,
seeking the sun and the warmth on our wings.
So perfectly patterned, so pretty, so powerful!
Onward and onward and onward until . . .

we arrive together, millions and millions.
We flit and we flutter, filling the forest,
until each tree is covered with our sunburst orange,
like a whole new set of leaves.

POND LIFE

Long back legs

like oars on a rowing boat,

the **water boatman**

paddles around the pond.

Up quick, to grab a breath,

the **diving beetle**

traps air beneath its wings,

like a scuba-diver's oxygen tank.

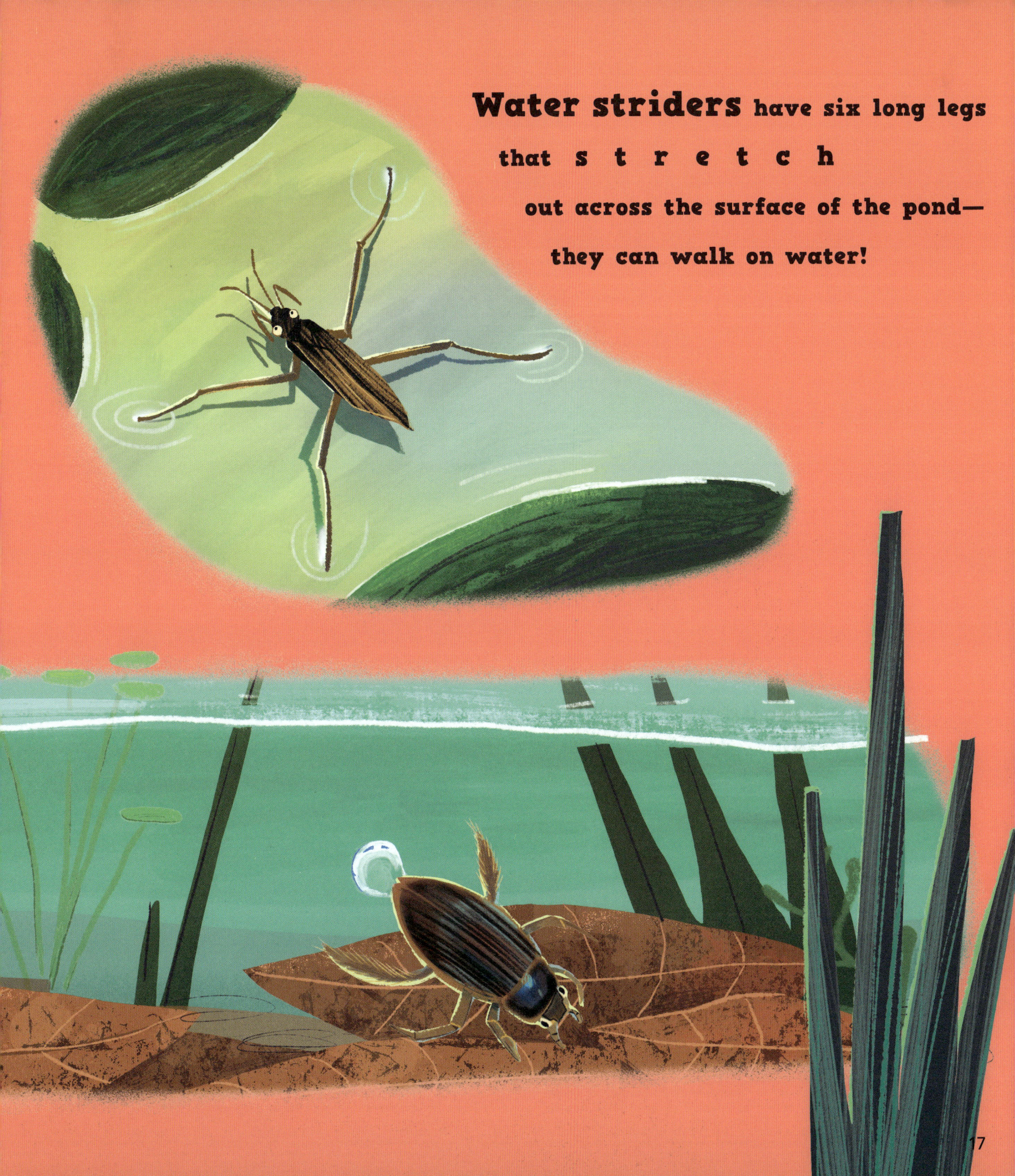

Water striders have six long legs that s t r e t c h out across the surface of the pond— they can walk on water!

17

WOODLICE

Under here it's damp and dark.
Just how we like it!

Soggy moss and moldy leaves.
Just how we like it!

Under here there are loads of us.
Just how we—

EEEEEEK! NO! THE LOG IS BEING LIFTED!

Roly-poly, tuck up tight.

Curl up small, into a ball,

as tiny as a pea.

STAG BEETLES

The beetle battle.

The big beetle battle.

The big beetle battle on the branch—

UP HERE!

The beetle battle.
The big beetle battle.
The big beetle battle on the branch—
OH DEAR!

COCKROACHES

Your skeleton is inside your body,
but my skeleton is on the *outside*.
A super-suit of armor,
flexible and tough enough
to stop me from getting crushed
by 900 times my own body weight!

That's about the same as a seven-year-old child

being absolutely fine

if you stacked up

five **African elephants** on top of them.

BOMBARDIER BEETLES

Hey, froggy! Stay back!

Or it's POP! POP! POP!

You're looking at a beetle

with a gun on its butt,

and right now, I'm loading up

a bubbling bomb-blast explosion in my gut.

Rapid fire! Twenty shots!

Super-scorcher! Ultra-hot!

One more move and I will shoot!

Scorching, scalding, TOXIC juice!

Hey, froggy! Stay back!

Or it's POP! POP! POP!

POP! POP! POP!

BEAUTIFUL BEASTS

ORB WEAVER SPIDERS

There's a spider in this poem, and it won't get out!

I tried to write about beautiful sunsets and rainbows . . .

but somehow, there it was. The spider.

Scuttling around in my poem. This poem.

I tried to sweep it out with a dustpan and brush.

And, at first, I thought it had worked . . .

but no luck! There it was, spinning

the beginnings of a sticky little web.

One silk thread flung out on the wind

like a tightrope. The spider just danced right across.

And then—spiral after spiral—just look at this spider!

So totally at home in my poem about beautiful things.

SAND SCORPIONS

Back and forth! Back and forth!

Like dance partners holding hands—

or deadly enemies fighting.

SNAILS

When it's good and wet and rainy,
I might climb right up your window.
You can watch me from inside
as I squeeze and then relax
tiny lines of mighty muscles
in a wondrous wave . . .

and as it ripples down my body,
those tiny lines of mighty muscles
push me forward, drag me onward.

It might take me a while,
but it's good and wet and rainy,
and you're watching from inside.
And there's nothing else to look at
that's quite like me.

NEW ZEALAND GLOW-WORMS

Ooh! Look at those fairy lights,

sparkling like stars in a perfect night sky . . .

Oh no, hold on, it's actually snot! Deadly snot,

dangling down from the tail of a glow-worm,

like a fishing line looking for a catch.

A sticky string of tiny slime balls,

with such a beautiful blue-green glow

that passing flies and gnats can't resist

a closer look. Closer and closer and . . .

TANGLED! TRAPPED! NOW YOU'RE A SNACK!

PART OF THE JOB!

Whether it's being **nibbled** by a lizard

or **gobbled** by a frog,

for a bug, being **eaten** is part of the job!

It could be **breakfast** for a bird

or a **snack** for a snake.

It could be **brunch** for a bat at the back of a cave.

No bugs—no lizards!

No bugs—no bats!

No bugs—no birds!

It's as simple as that!

No bugs—no snakes!

No bugs—no frogs!

For a bug, being **eaten**

is part of the job!

MAYFLIES

One year

under water.

Now, up to the surface.

Hatch out! Fly away! They just get

one day.

SLUGS

A slug can crawl,

or rather slide,

all along

the sharpest side

of the sharpest sword

and not get cut

or hurt one bit!

The super-slime

that helps it stick

and climb up walls

also makes it smooth enough

to glide along the roughest stuff

and not get cut

or hurt one bit!

GOLIATH BIRDEATER TARANTULAS

Some advice for the mice: *Stay home! Lay low!*

There's a spider out here, with fangs as long as cheetahs' claws!

Stealthy. Silent. Oh. So. Still. Until . . .

A wiggle of your whiskers

    sends a ripple through the air.

        Super-sensor leg hairs tingle,

           so now it knows you're there.

Pounce! Grab! Stab quick! Jab the venom in!

Some advice for the mice: *Stay home! Lay low!*

COOL CATERPILLARS

Some are bright green, with venomous spines that can hurt you.
Some disguise themselves as dangerous snakes—or as bird poo!

Some look stranger than you could dream up or imagine,
like a cross between an alien, a slug, and a dragon . . .

Some cling to twigs so you can't shake them off.
Or have horns that look deadly but are actually soft.

Some can eat three times their own weight in a day!
But the coolest thing about them all? Well, that's over THIS WAY . . .

CHRYSALIS

Safe inside a shiny suit of armor,

I melt myself down and start over again.

Feeding on the soupy goo

that I made from myself.

It's like magic! The way that I change—

from a small squishy alien-thingy with legs

to a perfectly patterned sky-flutterer.

Watch as the chrysalis splits,

and I open my wings

for the very first time.

WORKING TOGETHER

LEAFCUTTER ANTS

We're a team of five million farmers.

All day gathering leaves we don't eat—
hoisted high above our heads like giant green flags.

Back home, we chop the leaves up smaller,
to make a compost full of goodness
that we use to grow a fungus.
Just like you might grow some veggies
in a garden or a farm.

And this massive, white fungus,
soft as butter, twice as tasty . . .
It makes all the hard work worth it!

We feed the fungus and the fungus feeds us!

POTATO BUGS

We bang a beat with our bellies,

bang a beat with our bellies,

bang a beat on the ground down below . . .

Hello! Hello! Anybody here?

Hit and bash in different patterns,

drumming till the earth shakes,

calling out for somebody we know . . .

Hello! Hello! Anybody here?

52

Yes! I get the message, loud and clear!

LADYBUGS

If a spotted little creepy creature's sucking sap from leaves,

munching cauliflower and cucumber and everything between . . .

If there's pesky pests all over all your peas and lima beans . . .

Then you need a ladybug!

A ladybug is what you need!

A ladybug to eat the beasties that are eating up your greens,
to chase the aphids off the broccoli and keep your eggplants clean.
If what you want is pest control—a bug-munching machine . . .

Then you need a ladybug!

A ladybug is what you need!

HOME

Home can be beautiful!

Built up by Mom's endless efforts

scooping and carrying mud—just for you.

Patting and smoothing down mud—just for you.

MUD DAUBER
WASP

Home can be huge!

Tunnels and rooms, connected inside,

the tiniest teammates, all working together,

can make something so massive!

CATHEDRAL
TERMITES

Home can be carried around with you!
Twigs carefully chosen and stacked
in a pattern, spiraling up
to a perfect point.

BAGWORM
MOTHS

BUMBLEBEES

Flower after flower.
Buzz, buzz, buzz.

Pack the pollen,
   nab the nectar.
      Glug, glug, glug.
     Nab the nectar,
pack the pollen.

Buzz, buzz, buzz.
Flower after flower.

EARTHWORMS

Wriggle-wriggle-dig! Wriggle-dig-dig-wriggle!
Dig up all the worms—whether big or little!

All plants need water and air to grow,

and these little pink squiggles

wriggle-dig-dig tunnels in the ground,

so the water drip-drips . . . trick-trickles . . . deep down,

so the air has space down there to move around.

And the plants grow taller, quicker, bigger.

Wriggle-wriggle-dig! Wriggle-dig-dig-digger!

DRAGONFLIES

Even when the wind blows blustery surprises,

I can fly side to side, zip forward, or reverse,

even stop—just there—in midair.

They say I hover like a helicopter.

They say I fly like a drone.

But really it's the other way around!

I've inspired inventors

to imagine new flying machines . . .

Ideas lifting off in different directions—just like I do.

WITHOUT FLIES

We'd be knee-deep in steaming heaps of poop!

We'd be sinking into mountains of moldy, mulchy leaves!

Flies feed on all the stinky stuff we don't want left around.

Flies are a clean-up crew that helps the plants grow.

Some people think that flies are gross,

but the world would be SO MUCH grosser without them!

GRASSHOPPERS

Can you hear them yet? The grasshoppers are calling!

Rubbing their legs against their wings

to sing out to each other.

The field fizzes with chirps and clicks.

It sounds a bit like somebody shaking a shaker

next to someone else shaking a shaker.

And I know that their song is only for each other,

but I like to think they know I'm listening too.

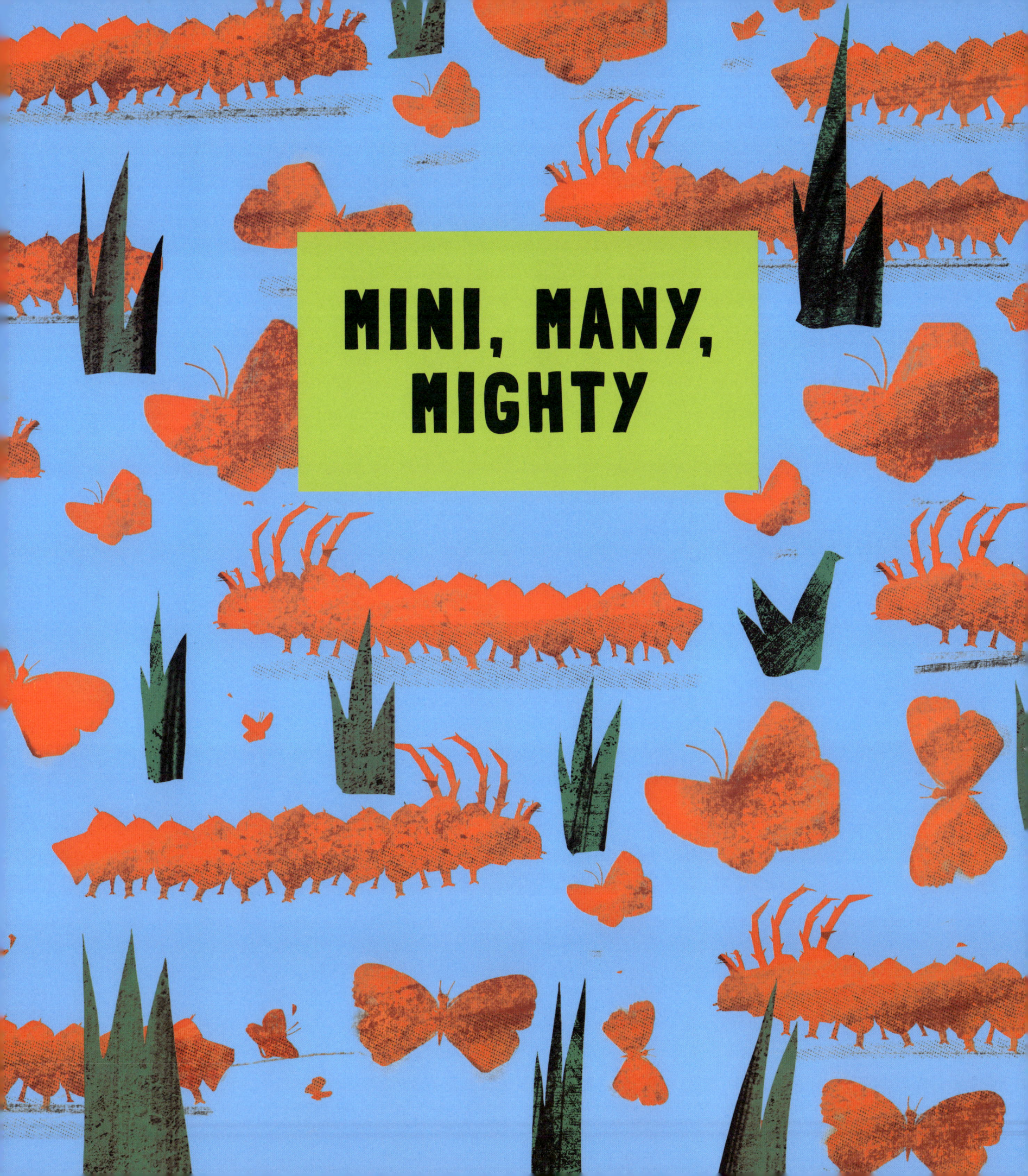

MINI, MANY, MIGHTY

WHO'S WHO?

In this book, we've met many insects and other tiny creatures. There are over a million different types of bugs around the world, and scientists think there are many more yet to be discovered. To help us study them, we group bugs into different categories. If you want to identify a bug, a good place to start is by asking, "Is it an insect?"

BEE

FLY

BEETLE

INSECTS

Most of the bugs in this book are insects. Did you know that there are more types of insect than any other animal group?
All insects have:
- six legs
- a body with three segments
- a hard outer layer called an exoskeleton
- antennae on their head

ANT

LADYBUG

GRASSHOPPER

NOT INSECTS

Gastropods have a lot fewer legs than insects! These soft-bodied creatures sometimes have a shell. Many gastropods live underwater, but the two in this book don't!

SLUG

SNAIL

Myriapods often have a lot more legs than insects! Centipedes and millipedes may look similar to each other, but centipedes are speedy hunters and millipedes are slow leaf-munchers.

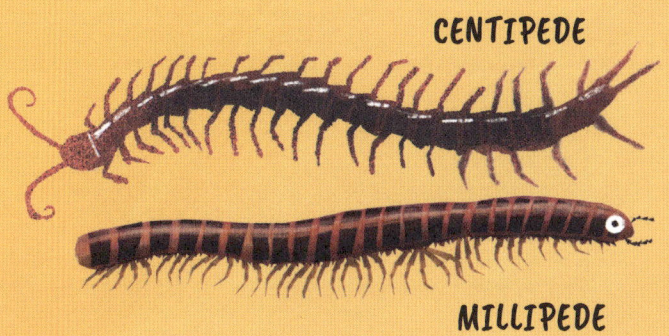

CENTIPEDE

MILLIPEDE

Annelids are soft-bodied creatures that are divided into segments. They live all over the world—in soil, oceans, and freshwater environments.

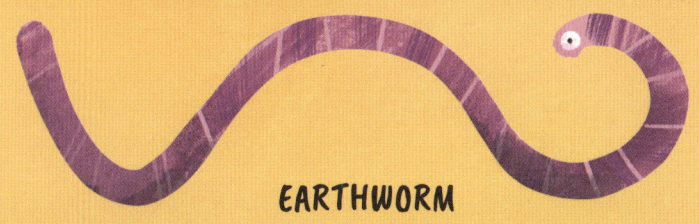

EARTHWORM

Arachnids might look similar to insects, but there are some key differences to look out for! All arachnids have:
- eight legs
- a body with two segments
- no antennae

GOLIATH BIRDEATER TARANTULA

SAND SCORPION

ORB WEAVER SPIDER

Crustaceans have a hard shell and several pairs of legs and are usually sea creatures, like lobsters or crabs. Woodlice are the only crustaceans that live their whole lives on land.

WOODLOUSE

BUGS ARE AMAZING

Bugs keep the world working. Whether they crawl, fly, scuttle, or slither, bugs get the job done. Let's take a closer look at a few of the amazing ways that bugs help to support life on Earth.

Flower friends!
Super-powered pollinators!

Some bugs carry a sticky substance called pollen from flower to flower as they feed. This helps the plants to form seeds, which in turn grow into new plants.

Bat breakfast!
A snack that you can save for later!

Did you know that bugs play a vital role in the food web? These tiny creatures are the sole food source for many amphibians, reptiles, birds, and mammals. Without bugs, many creatures could not survive.

Garbage-gobblers, munching up mold!

Lots of bugs are natural decomposers. By feeding on dead plant materials and dead animals, bugs perform a valuable service as Earth's clean-up crew. These garbage-gobblers also send important nutrients back into the soil and help to keep it healthy.

All hail the garden guardians! The legendary leaf patrol!

Some bugs eat smaller bugs that would like to eat our plants. Ladybugs, hoverflies, and some wasps act as natural pest control, helping to guard our gardens!

So now that we know a bit more about how bugs help us, let's turn the page to find out how we can help THEM!

HOW TO BE A BUG-LOVER

Bugs are essential to life on Earth—but these little creatures are under threat, and their numbers are dwindling. So how do we protect them? Here are a few things that bug lovers can do to help these cool critters to thrive.

Stone-turners, leaf-lifters, log-rollers, pond-dippers!

You can find bugs almost anywhere—from fields and forests to balconies and back gardens. Scientists have predicted that there are millions more bugs yet to be discovered, so get out your magnifying glass and see if you can find the next species!

Note-takers, close-uppers, wing-watchers, bug-lovers!

Now that you know how to tell which bug is which, you can take part in a bug survey. Make sure you note down the names and numbers of bugs you find, and then you can come back to the same place again and again to see if the numbers have grown!

Seed-planters, stick-stackers, re-wilders, grow-backers!

Looking after bug habitats is a great way to care for these little creatures. You can even do this at home—planting nectar-rich flowers in a window box or a garden. Why not make a bug hotel filled with dry leaves, dead wood, and hollow tubes? This will make an ideal home for beetles, centipedes, spiders, and more.

BUG HOTEL

Letter-writers, banner-wavers, brave-chanters, bug-savers!

Be a bug champion! As well as making changes in our own lives, we can spread awareness about the importance of protecting bugs. With your help, they can continue to be the thriving force for good that they are.

MINI, MANY, MIGHTY

All shapes and all sizes, bugs come in myriads.

Some fill this whole page, some fit in this period.

WE ARE MINI!

Some line up in a team of twenty million.

Some fill a whole forest with their bright orange brilliance.

WE ARE MANY!

Some can carry more than 1,000 times their own weight.

Some help plants to grow, putting food on your plate.

Bugs were here way before the days of the dinosaur,

and they're still here now, so hear them roar . . .

WE ARE MINI, WE ARE MANY,
WE ARE MIGHTY!

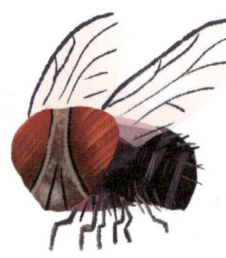

For Ivan and Frances—thank you for all your help with these poems. You're not quite as mini as you were when I started writing this book, but you are definitely still mega mighty!

SM

For Zelda

AM

With thanks to Dr. Nick C. Crumpton for his expertise and advice. Thank you to David Clarke at London Zoo and Emily Greig at Berkshire College of Agriculture for showing me some real-life bugs.

First US edition 2025
First published by Walker Books Ltd. (UK) 2025

Library of Congress Control Number: pending
ISBN 978-1-5362-3887-7

25 26 27 28 29 30 CCP 10 9 8 7 6 5 4 3 2 1

Printed in Shenzhen, Guangdong, China

This book was typeset in HVD Comic Serif, Avenir Next, and Caveat Brush.
The illustrations were done in mixed media.

Candlewick Press
99 Dover Street
Somerville, Massachusetts 02144

www.candlewick.com

EU Authorized Representative: HackettFlynn Ltd, 36 Cloch Choirneal, Balrothery, Co. Dublin, K32 C942, Ireland. EU@walkerpublishinggroup.com